Secret Postin
Bletchley Park to the

Charlotte Webb

For a fellow Veteran!

Charlotte We bb,

BookTower
PUBLISHING

First published by BookTowerPublishing 2011
Redditch, Worcestershire
www.booktowerpublishing.co.uk

1 2 3 4 5 6 7 8 9 10

A catalogue record for this book is available from the British
Library

ISBN 978-0-9557164-1-6

Printed and bound in Great Britain by
PrintondemandWorldwide

Set in Georgia font pt 9 & 10

For my parents
Without their love, help and encouragement my life would
have been the poorer.

Contents

Acknowledgements

Without a great deal of encouragement and help this insight into the past would not have been possible. Therefore my grateful thanks go to members of my family, Judith Frames and Kerry Johnson.

Foreword

Although this is mainly a personal record spanning the major part of a century, readers may find it interesting to compare the relatively simple way in which we lived before the advent of the many forms of 'must have' equipment, such as washing machines, dishwashers, telephones, computers etc, which most of us take for granted today. Looking back over the last eighty plus years, I realise how fortunate I am to have lived through such interesting and progressive times.

Chapter 1

Civilian to Service

Thinking back I can see myself as an eighteen year old listening to the news on the wireless, wishing I could do more for the war effort. That May afternoon was the start of a journey that would take me to the Government Code and Cypher School's covert operation at Bletchley Park and then, after the European war had ended in May 1945, on to the Pentagon in Washington D.C to see out the remainder of the war against Japan.

It was May 1941 and the bombing of Britain, known as the Blitz, had ended. I was halfway through a Domestic Science Course at Radbrook College near Shrewsbury to learn how cook, run a house and do household accounts. It was hard to focus when the Blitz had seen the destruction or damage to over one million homes since September 1940. Due to food shortages, it was also difficult to remain enthusiastic about cooking colourless food from simplified war time recipes.

During the two terms I had been at Radbrook there was a growing restlessness and for some of us our daily lives became increasingly frustrating. For me, illness exacerbated my dissatisfaction during which a bout of measles and chickenpox meant a period of isolation with only 'Gone With The Wind' by Margaret Mitchell as refuge against the boredom. It was listening to the bad news of the war on the wireless that day in

May that fuelled my dissatisfaction and inspired me to leave the course and join up. Four of us chose to leave – surely we could contribute more to the War effort?

At that time, joining the Women's Services was voluntary as conscription of women had not started and I had to choose between the Auxiliary Territorial Service (ATS), Women's Royal Naval Service (WRNS) or the Women's Auxiliary Air Force (WAAF) without understanding the function each service provided. I made my choice based on the qualifications I had gained through home schooling and, like many other women, the attractiveness of the service uniform! Based on those criteria, my first choice was the popular WRNS but there were no vacancies, so I applied and was accepted for the ATS.

Established by Royal Warrant on 9 September 1938 the ATS was part of the British Army and was initially attached to the Territorial Army. By the time I joined on 3 September 1941, the ATS had been granted full military status and there were sixty five thousand of us serving our country. The military status ensured that officers received a commission and rank in the same way as the male officers, but unfortunately we did not get equal pay. As more men joined the war, more women volunteered but the continued pressure to support the war effort prompted the coming into force of the National Service Act in December 1941, which called up all unmarried women between the ages of twenty and thirty years old to join one of the women's services. By September 1943 the number of women serving in the ATS peaked at 212,500 before the numbers began to decline gradually until the end of the war. The ATS was disbanded in 1949 and replaced on 1 February 1949 by the Women's Royal Army Corps (WRAC).

Chapter 2

Life in the Countryside

Life in the ATS came as a big culture shock for me. Growing up in Richard's Castle, a village four and a half miles from Ludlow in the scenic Herefordshire Countryside was a million miles away from living in close quarters with hundreds of other girls, where space and privacy were rare.

My clearest childhood memory dates back to September 1927 about the time I was four years of age and my brother David died. I had been staying in the village with the Hall family, who often 'gave a hand' as David had struggled with ill health since his birth on 31 January 1925. On walking back up the front path to the family home, 'Ryecroft', I asked *'where is David?'* and was told to *'ssh'*. I think I sensed that he had died but I cannot remember how I coped after then.

'Ryecroft' is the name of the three acres of grassland raised above Woodhouse Lane that made up our family home. From the bungalow we looked out onto an extensive view from Clee Hill (Titterstone) in the east along to Abberley, and Stoke Edith. The property was, and still is, surrounded by many trees – Copper Beech, Spanish and Horse Chestnut, Norwegian Spruce, Yew and many varieties of fruits and shrubs. We lived on our own fruit and vegetable crops, a small apiary, goats, pigs and poultry. There was no gas, electricity nor mains water, so heating was by open coal or wood fires and water was pumped from a well under the bungalow. Cooking was by Valor paraffin stoves and lighting by paraffin lamps and candles.

The latrines at Ryecroft were quite a walk from the house, which was not funny when it was pouring with rain or one needed to go in a hurry! The journey took you from the back door, along the hedge adjacent to the house, past the back of the bee hives to the honeysuckle covered privy. The building was covered by an enormous yew tree, hiding its existence to those not knowing where to look.

Groceries were delivered from Ludlow every two weeks. Messrs. Stephens travelled round collecting the orders one week and delivering the next. A bus ran in and out of Ludlow, stopping at every house if needed, twice on Saturdays and once on Mondays. It was used mainly by cottagers and small-holders taking their produce to Ludlow market.

My Father, who was employed by Lloyds Bank, commuted to Ludlow by motor cycle and in deep snow he walked! We did not get a family car until 1938 so when we needed to travel by train we were taken by pony and trap, driven by Jack Pugh, a local farmer to Woofferton Station, a busy junction on the Great Western Railway (GWR) lines to Birmingham and the North South line between Crewe and Bristol. I can still remember the intense cold and feel the stinging chilblains which enveloped us on the pony and trap trips.

What we lacked in 'mod cons' was more than compensated for in the lush countryside, the fresh air and freedom of the open space. I remember that I slept in a tent in the garden most of the summer free from worries about thieves, traffic and noise. On fine nights I took my bed out so that I could lie and gaze at the stars and try to comprehend the infinite distances.

Our problems tended to be weather related. There seemed to be more snow in those days and it lodged in the corrugated iron roof gables and seeped through into the bedrooms. Then, often, there were droughts in the summers when the well dried up and so did the waterbutts. A bowl of clean water was used to wash the vegetables, then the dishes and finally on to plants in the garden. Daily bathing was out of the question during long droughts.

My sister, Margaret, arrived in the night of 29 September 1930 in the bedroom next to mine. The following year Mother had a mastectomy and subsequently had to have radium treatment in Birmingham. She was one of the first women to survive the operation. We were fortunate; there were always lads and lassies available to do jobs in the house and garden. There was much poverty and people were glad of a meal as payment for work. We also had an au pair from Germany (Tante Moderau) in the early thirties and later Clara Mandli (now Buchmann) from Zurich. She rang me on 13 May 2008 from an old people's home – I believe she was ninety six at the time.

Mother must have had an iron will for she carried on with so much for thirty years before she died: coping with the animals, teaching us and doing endless charitable things in the village including setting up basket making classes using the osiers, a species of willow we grew to teach unemployed men in the village to make a living out of basket-making.

She was an organist, pianist and singer and played classical pieces for us to go to sleep with every evening. She taught us to play the piano. We also had violin lessons. I found the violin very difficult and could have been a better pianist if I had worked harder at it – but if nothing else I learned to appreciate good music and it is still part of my life. Mother sang in a choir conducted by Sir Edward Elgar.

We were educated under the Parents National Educational Union (PNEU) System which covered a broad spectrum of subjects. We also had private tuition with Miss Faraday (a niece of Michael Faraday, the scientist). I was *hopeless* at exams and never achieved any good results, apart from being able to speak fairly good German and I taught myself Spanish which has been quite useful with translating the Spanish edition of the Organisation of American States Magazine, shopping in Spain and Tenerife as well as trying to understand my hairdresser in Chile – I must say that was the most difficult! To me the Chilean Spanish has quite a dialect.

In his spare time, Dad worked hard in the garden and we had all the fruit and vegetables one could possibly want. His main hobby was cricket and he played for the Ludlow and South Shropshire team for whom Mother would often provide afternoon tea for the players with homemade bread and cakes. The cricket ground was about 8 miles from home – far enough on a bicycle with the provisions in the basket!

Many of the farms and cottages were part of the Moor Park Estate, nestled in the countryside between Richard's Castle and Ludlow, or belonged to the former Lord of the Manor, Mr Roger Salwey, whose family goes back many hundred years: I recall one of their gravestones in the old village churchyard, St Bartholomew's, dated 1500. Lancing College was evacuated to Moor Park during World War II, following which it was sold off and has continued to be used as a school.

In the new village church, All Saints, we had our allocated seats — the Salweys in the front row of the left hand aisle, behind them Captain Ronnie Wallace and the Kennedy family from the Lodge, and the Windsor-Clives (Clive of India). We sat behind them. On the right hand side the Betton-Fosters and the Alcock family had pride of place and the rest of the community sat behind them.

The organ needed water to activate the bellows and the supply came from Boney Well which was not always consistent because some of the houses between the well and the church were also supplied from the same pipeline. Mrs Alcock played for the services: Leipzig Conservatoire trained, she was excellent. Mother played the organ from time to time, putting her music talent to good use.

Chapter 3

In the Time of War

Dad joined the Royal West Kent Regiment as an Army Officer direct from school (Rochester King's School) in 1914. He served in Mesopotamia (re-named Iraq) and India, returning to the UK in 1918.

Sometime between 1918 and my parent's wedding in 1920 he began working for Lloyds Bank in Ludlow. They lived in 'The Villa' in Aston on Clun, where I was born.

An active member of the local branch of the British Legion, he was selected to serve in 1938 in the British Legion Police Force in Czechoslovakia. The mission was aborted within weeks – Dad's report on this, in full, can be found at the back of this book.

Mother had been a music teacher in a school in Germany for a year from August 1914 until August 1915. World War I broke out on the 4 August 1914, the day Mother travelled to Germany and arrived at the school near Leipzig. No attempt to stop her was made at customs, nor was she turned back upon arrival. However, she was classed as the enemy and obliged to report to the local police station each day, although as time went by the police became quite friendly and simply acknowledged her with a wave each day. After a year's negotiations with the American Embassy in Berlin she was granted safe passage to return to the UK. Unfortunately, we never had the opportunity to talk more about her time there.

Passport from Germany, 1914 © Charlotte Webb

My first experience of Germany came in 1937 through an exchange visit with Elisabeth Paul (pronounced Powell), who came from a little town called Herrnhut in Saxony, near Dresden. She came to us for three months through the summer to improve her English and for me to improve my German by staying with her family in Germany. Elisabeth and I were of a similar age but from very different backgrounds.

The journey started from Ludlow on a train to London where my great uncle Cecil Stockton met us and gave us a whistle stop tour of London to fill the hours until our next train to Harwich. As a London resident Uncle Cecil showed us the sites with which he was very familiar. I had a lot of luggage because (at that time) it was customary for washing to be done every six weeks so it was necessary to take six of every item of underwear. From Harwich we boarded a ferry to Flushing (Holland). The final leg of the overnight train journey to Dresden was very tiring and very uncomfortable. I couldn't sleep and felt rather miserable. After four days on the way it was a relief to arrive in Dresden where Elisabeth's mother met us and showed us something of the city. We went to a historical jousting tournament before going on to the Paul family home in Herrnhut.

I felt very homesick and miserable throughout the journey, which was about a thousand miles. Elisabeth's family and Tante Moderau met us and we moved on to the Paul family home in Herrnhut where I lived and went to school. I soon settled down and began to enjoy my visit. My German was reasonable but not good enough to do essays or exams.

Herrnhut had a very strong Moravian (Brudergemeine) community – very religious. Traditionally men and women sat separately on opposite sides of church during church services and the women wore significant bonnets. Widows wore black bonnets, married women wore blue and singles, pink. The 'Bonnets' were made of a pretty netting and tied under the chin with ribbons.

It was a very quiet, understated community and their clothing rather similar to English styles, except the bonnets. I do remember that they had a sort of duvet, similar to what is commonly used today. At home, at that time we were still using sheets and blankets. It was common in German houses to have a solid fuel Ofen – an enclosed stove in the centre of the room. The family lived high up in a block of flats with a balcony overlooking the green surrounding landscape. There also seemed to be a shortage of butter. I know not why!

(From left) Elisabeth & Erdmuth Paul, Charlotte Vine-Stevens, 1937 © Charlotte Webb

During my stay I was included in many of their social activities including family weddings and christenings. I also attended school, which started at 7am and ended at 1.30pm. The afternoons were always filled with sports. One particular day stands out in my mind when the school went to a farm on the Czech border to harvest potatoes – I was stiff the next day.

In school we were obliged to stand to attention and give the Hitler salute at the beginning and end of every class. Herrnhut was the main Brudergemeine (Moravian church), which exists in several other countries including Great Britain. I did not fully comprehend the German threat but felt it was diplomatic to join in with the class requirement to salute. I disguised my discomfort by waving my arms but not joining the verbal salute. I certainly felt an undercurrent of concern.

Herr Paul did try to convey to me the local anxiety about the political situation and Hitler regime but my German was not good enough to fully understand his words. Elisabeth and Erdmuth aged fourteen and twelve were obliged to belong to the Bund Deutches Madels (as far as I could make out it was a very military set up). They disappeared every Sunday morning but I was not allowed to attend as a guest. I was aware that it was a requirement but Herr Paul and his wife were not happy that their children joined in. It was never discussed by the parents and Elisabeth never talked to me of it.

I remember an anxious time when Erdmut had scarlet fever and even though were all shared wooden bunks in the same room I was lucky enough not to catch it. On October 20th she went into Zittau Hospital on the Czech border. Although she was very ill she made a full recovery.

Living with the family and meeting their friends and relations was a good experience but I was glad to be home again. I kept in touch with the Paul family in Herrnhut until World War II broke out and did not hear from them again, which I regret.

I still have a postcard my host sent to my parents and brings back many fond memories of my time with his family:

"Dear Mr. Vine-Stevens
Herewith I thank you for the friendly sent views of Betty. Furthermore I confirm to you the receipt of the 50 deutschmark which I received in two traveller cheques from your bank, which I handed over to your daughter Betty. Betty is very happy with my 2 girls, especially Elisabeth, we see them often happy together. We, my wife and I, have become quite fond of Betty, as she integrates with our family and also helps my wife in the household. In school it seems that she understands almost everything well, her German speaking becomes better every day! We often play music together, which we all love a lot! We already look for a companion for the return journey for Betty. I myself have a lot of work to do with the creation of my business premises.

With best regards to you and your wife.

I am very sincerely

Gerhard Paul"

In the summer of 1938, we went on a rare family holiday to Fairbourne on the Welsh coast.. There I met my first 'boyfriend', Otto Stoetzer. I was fifteen and he seventeen. He was on holiday from Germany. Fluent in German, Spanish and French, I thought he was the 'bees knees' and was delighted to be able to air my German. We corresponded until war broke out and met again after the war but a lasting romance was not to be. However, he sent me the Spanish version of the

Organisation of American States Magazine regularly from Buenos Aires so I was able to keep up limited Spanish and learn a lot about South America and its problems.

In 1938 Dorothea Schiffer joined us from Breslau in Germany: her father was Jewish and a Doctor of Medicine. Her mother came from an aristocratic family (the von Braunschweigs) who died before Dorothea came away from the gathering Nazi regime. She soon became one of the family and stayed until training as a children's nurse in London. We remained good friends until she died in 1966 of cancer. I felt very lost without her and still do, but her daughter, Hella, whom I consider an adopted niece, is a delight and we are in close touch even though she and her family live on Barra in the Outer Hebrides.

As soon as War was declared on 3 September 1939, Dad became an officer in the Home Guard. He had a large area to oversee on the Herefordshire, Shropshire and Worcestershire borders. At least he had some petrol, but of course we could not use it unless we happened to be going where he was on duty!

Chapter 4

Training for War

The war changed many lives, and mine was no exception. It affected us in the country probably much less than those in our towns and cities. There was more to eat and while we often heard enemy planes passing overhead we were spared the horrors of bombing raids that devastated other towns and cities. We did see the flashes of light beyond Clee Hill as bombs fell on Birmingham over fifty miles away. Between April 1940 and August 1943 Birmingham became the third heaviest bombed city in the country.

My calling up papers for the ATS arrived in 1941 with instructions that I report to a training centre in Wrexham, North Wales for 'Basic Training'. I travelled by train from Ludlow on a train so cramped, it was standing room only. As the day vanished so did our light because of the blackouts and it was impossible to see where we were.

The training centre was situated within the Royal Welsh Fusiliers' barracks. Although in the same compound, we occupied separate areas from the men. On arrival we underwent a series of medical examinations and various anti viral injections, followed by our kit issue. The standard kit issue consisted of:

A khaki cap
A khaki skirt and tunic
Khaki shirts, collars and ties
Bras, vests, knickers, stockings
Shoes (beetle crushers!)

Tooth brush and shoe brushes
Pyjamas
Great coat and rain coat
Gas mask
Shoulder bag
Disposable sanitary towels

Charlotte Vine-Stevens in uniform, 1945 © Charlotte Webb

I enjoyed wearing uniform (even though it wasn't a very good fit); it was something to be proud of. A collar and tie was a totally new experience for me and the collar left a red painful mark on my neck. Learning to tie the tie took ages – but we helped each other out. The khaki knickers were so long for me that they either showed below my knees or if pulled up, the waist line ended under my armpits. Overall our kit was pretty rough but it served its purpose. The gas mask was heavy, compared with the civilian models and had to be carried at all times.

We were housed in wooden huts made up of basic standard military equipment – functional but not very comfortable. This was to be our home for the six week basic training as we were marched, paraded and assessed for intelligence and trade assignments by female drill sergeants.

Pay for a Private was ten shillings (50p) per week, which doesn't sound much but out of it we went to the cinema and were able to buy toiletries – sometimes. There was, of course, a shortage of everything. Later, at Bletchley Park I recall being able to buy one small bar of chocolate per week from the NAAFI.

Life in barracks was a complete culture shock for me. Girls from all walks of life and backgrounds rubbed shoulders, all learning to work as a team, all with a common purpose – to serve our country. It seems minor in the chaos of our lives, but the biggest shock came from viewing the social behaviour displayed by the girls and in particular the varied standard of table manners. Until that point I had naively believed everyone had lived as I had.

Some of my tasks were also an education. I remember I was given the unpleasant task of looking for lice – something I had never heard of. Those of the new recruits who were found to have lice were bandaged in paraffin-soaked head scarves but with so many girls living in close quarters the battle of head lice was not so easily won.

I particularly remember the gas mask drill where we were taken to a small room while wearing our gasmasks and a small amount of gas was released. We were then ordered to remove our gasmasks and everyone was instantly convulsed by coughing and spluttering as the gas entered our lungs. It taught us the importance of carrying our gasmasks at all times, taking gas warnings seriously and obeying procedure without question.

The quiet life in rural Herefordshire and home schooling had not equipped me for anything in particular beyond being able to communicate in reasonable colloquial German, which I learned through Mother and a number of Swiss and German 'au pairs' during my early years. My abandoned college course had only equipped me for running a family home so I arrived in Wrexham with no true understanding of what my skills were. It was an interesting time to find out just exactly what I could put my mind to.

I enjoyed the experience of my basic training and by the end I waited with trepidation to see which trade I would be assigned to. Every recruit was assessed and allocated a trade but not for me a posting as a cook, orderly, signal operator, driver, radar operator. No, I was ordered to an address in London which entailed an overnight journey in a very crowded train. I rolled up my great coat for a pillow and lay in the corridor for most of the journey. Of course there were no lights and it was difficult to see those around me. What a relief to arrive at Euston at 6.30a.m., deposit my kit bag in the Left Luggage office, walk to Piccadilly and have breakfast at Lyons

Corner House. Porridge was on the menu, but it did not taste as good as the brand I was used to – having been cooked overnight in our Aga.

It had been four years since the whirlwind tour of London in 1937. It seems ironic to me now that my first visit to the capital was as part of my journey to pre-war Germany, where I had received so much hospitality and my second visit, as part of my duty in the fight against Germany. London was still very grand despite the bomb damage of 1940. By today's standards there were hardly any civilians and very little traffic.

When I arrived at Devonshire House in Piccadilly I still had no idea why I was there. I was interviewed in German by a very pleasant twinkly-eyed Army Major from the Intelligence Corps. The interview was short and he did not tell me why I had been ordered there or what was expected of me. I was asked how I would communicate with someone in Scotland to which I responded I would do so by telephone, in writing, by telegram or by courier. There were also general questions about my family but nothing about my time in Germany in 1937. It seemed a strange interview as there was no discussion of my skills. I suspect it was a test of my overall intelligence, language skills and reliability.

I had obviously passed the interview but still did not know what was going on. My orders were to go to Euston railway station and take a train to Bletchley in the Buckinghamshire countryside where I would be met. It may now seem strange that I just followed my instructions without knowing my final destination or the reason for the journey but it was what I was trained to do, and did so willingly without any trepidation.

I was given a rail warrant and sent on my way with no further instructions. I collected my kit and boarded the train to Bletchley. Where Bletchley was, I had no idea! Another ATS girl, Wynn Angell, who was fluent in French, had also been directed to Bletchley. We began to talk and found we were heading to the same place. The train journey passed while listening to Wynn's description of her dramatic journey to Bletchley - she had recently escaped from Belgium (where the Germans had already taken over) and once in England she had joined the ATS keen to contribute to the war effort.

It was late by the time the train pulled up at Bletchley Station. Together we were taken to a civilian 'Billet' in Bradwell. It was a council house with three bedrooms already housing a family of four. Tired and hungry Wynn and I were directed to the room which would be ours, only to find we had to share a bed! Despite our embarrassment, sheer exhaustion won over and we slept.

Chapter 5

Bletchley Park

Bletchley Park - Pencil drawing by Mark Pettifer ©2009

It was September 1941 and I awoke in a strange bed, in a strange house with absolutely no idea the reason why I was there. After getting ready Wynn and I walked to the end of the drive and, as instructed, caught the coach transporting thirty or so people to Bletchley. We travelled the five miles to a destination which was still unknown to us. I still had no concept of where I was once I arrived at Bletchley Park. It was a large ugly house, surrounded by a well guarded perimeter.

The bus drove us along the drive to the mansion where we were dropped off and led into the small office next to the library where we were given the Official Secrets Act to read and swear we would abide by. I remember it was a vast document to read on the spot but its seriousness was very clearly pointed out to us. In short, that any and all information we read or heard within Bletchley Park must NEVER be talked about outside the department we were assigned to and not for thirty years after the end of hostilities.

An Army Captain oversaw our induction and his emphasis of the implications of breaking our silence remains with me today. There were degrees of punishment to fit the severity of any betrayal – the most serious being the death penalty. Looking at the gun lying beside the Captain, I realised the extreme seriousness of the duty with which I had been entrusted.

I felt at a loss at how I was to conduct myself. I took the decision that the only way forward was to say nothing outside of my office. As time went on I found that the new found reserve influenced my personality in that I was and still am more discreet about my own life. I found, as many of us did, our social conversations were flippant and inconsequential.

On that first day, it became clear that *no-one* could be told where I was – not even my parents. Letters were to be addressed to a Post Office Box number in London. I could phone out but not receive calls. This was totally unexpected and came as a real shock - while at Bletchley I was 'cut off'. However, we could travel about on leave days and I did go home from time to time, or have a day in London, Oxford, Cambridge or Bedford. My family readily accepted my situation and never asked me any awkward questions. Dad was ex-Army and therefore knew better than to ask.

So, 'fate' had taken me to the Government Code and Cypher School (GC&CS) for the duration of the Second World War. I was one of thousands drawn from our universities, our three services, civil servants and local men and women, all working on the painstaking process of breaking the various codes in German, Italian and Japanese in order to find out those countries' military moves and intentions.

WORK DUTIES

Bletchley, with its nine to ten thousand employees was a unique organisation and a unique experience. It is probably fair to say that every class of people in this country was represented. But we were a team of trustworthy individuals who had an important job to do – even though at the time we did not know the full story and 'small fry' like me did not ask!

Promotion at Bletchley was automatic – there were no tests or interviews, our rank progressed so that our pay was comparable with the civilians.

After signing the Official Secrets Act I was taken up the stairs to Major Tester's department. Wynn was taken somewhere else, possibly one of the huts but we never discussed it. I was put straight to work.

My first duties were in Major Ralph Tester's department which had rooms in the Mansion above the Ballroom. The four rooms were fairly small, and had possibly been servants' quarters in the time of the Leon family. I shared a small room with three men, which contained a desk for each of us and an open fire as the only heating source. The fire was only used at night but even then, we found there was insufficient fuel to last the colder nights. The room was rather claustrophobic, but we could see out over Hut 4 at the side of the mansion.

My duties were registering the morse code messages as they came in from the 'Y' (signal) stations, either by despatch rider or teleprinter. The registering of each message by date and call sign order was necessary for the decoders and translators to make quick reference. After registration, the messages were decoded, translated, transcribed and assessed according to urgency and then forwarded appropriately i.e. the Prime Minister, Commanders in the field or both. We worked a shift pattern 8am-4pm, 4pm-midnight, midnight-8am. Sounds easy – but it was tiring!

Major Tester was a nice, fatherly man who spoke perfect German and was engaged in translating at a very high level, particularly as he was also an expert in idiomatic German. After working with him for some time, he gave me a little test to see if my German was good enough to help with translations – he gently told me it was NOT!! (At least I tried). So I continued with three others to sort and register the morse code messages which came in vast quantities each day. It is said that many thousand a day were received – so there must have been another department which also registered them, we three could not have coped with the lot.

In a very small room next to mine worked a retired Colonel Thompson who had served with my Uncle Rex Vine-Stevens in the Royal Marine Engineers. Colonel Thompson recognised my name and introduced himself.

I remember two of the three men I shared an office with – Tubby Rootes, A Company Sergeant Major and a chap named Le Mesurier, whose christian name I do not recall. This is not unusual as we were generally referred to by our surnames. Every Wednesday morning Tubby Rootes relieved the most unpleasant twenty minutes set aside for the weekly gas mask drill. His rendition of 'In the Mood' with his gas mask on made the most hilarious bubbling sound.

In 1943/1944 when it became necessary to increase the number of staff in the Japanese Section I was transferred there in the newly built Block F (now demolished). My duties there included paraphrasing translated Japanese messages. My section head was C.J.W (Don) Parkin, a Foreign Office official. It was considered a precaution to paraphrase messages which we had picked up and decoded, so that if when we were passing on details of impending Japanese troop movements in Burma and they picked up our transmissions giving details of an impending counter attack, they could not be certain that we had broken their codes.

The paraphrased messages were sent in an inner and outer envelope, each with a coded address. I believe they were taken to a destination by despatch riders, but I did not know to whom.

Tabulated examples of translated messages and the paraphrased version	
Translated Intercepted Message	**Paraphrased Version of the Message**
London will be the target for night bombing on Tuesday 11 October.	The target is to be the Capital on October 11 after dark.
Troops of 3rd Battalion will be moved to attach Kohima in 3 days time.	Expect Kohima to be attacked 3 days from now by battalion strength.
The road between Meiktila and Kohima will be blocked on Monday to Thursday by tanks.	Road from Meiktila to Kohima to be out of use for 4 days due to tanks assembling.
Division stationed Meiktila will attack from East – Mon May 1st.	Expect attack early May, to west, probably Jap division 10.

I enjoyed getting my teeth into more 'meaty' work within the Japanese Section, but I appreciate how crucial to the process my previous task of registration was, even if it was dull.

The Japanese Section in Block F was a large section made up of four offices served by a central passageway and comprised of army and civilian personnel (ATS and Intelligence Corps staff) working twenty four hours over three shifts. There were three ATS girls in my office and the change from working with men for three years went off without a hitch. Our office was terribly cramped; we had a desk each with a typewriter. The only other furniture I recall is some sort of filing cabinet that had to be locked at the end of each shift.

Don Parkin was in the office next to mine. He was a very kindly man, easy to get on with and made working for him very pleasant. His wife was a WAAF sergeant and she would often call into the office for him. She must have also worked in the Japanese Section because coming to call for him from a different section would have been a breach of the security rules.

RECREATION

Duties permitting, there were plenty of recreational activities to take part in, such as a drama group, gramophone club, a madrigal group or Bach choir concerts under Herbert Murrill, (who was a professional singer and was employed by one of the radio stations after the war) and concerts given by the RAF Griller String Quintet. Towards the end of the war, after six hundred American servicemen had joined Bletchley Park, dances were laid on, with American refreshments which were, of course, a great treat.

Lectures were often given that were free to attend. The park grounds also formed part of our recreation time. If it was fine weather we would sit by the lake or walk around the grounds. One year there was heavy snowfall and people could be seen ice skating on the lake. Once I had left the billet in Loughton and went into the military camp on Shenley Road, there was also darts and my favourite game, table tennis. There was even a bar, but very rarely anything to drink.

Although we did not have lots of free time the varied social occasions made it easy to find new friends among others who were well aware of not being able to talk about our work. Things were a little trickier with friends outside of the park!

Soon after I arrived at Bletchley my parents introduced me to a handsome Canadian, who served in the Royal Canadian Air Force (RCAF). He was based at Biggin Hill, a large aerodrome in the south of England and we would meet in London and see shows and enjoy restaurant meals. One time he decided to surprise me and turned up in London unannounced and without the knowledge that the PO Box number on our correspondence was not my actual address. He arrived to be faced with nothing more than the post box system.

He was fun to be with and I enjoyed his company but the relationship did not last. Although he was keen to pursue our relationship I did not feel sufficient spark to tempt me with the possibility of going to Canada once the war was over.

I became good friends with a Junior Commander, Helen Mary Little through our mutual enjoyment of music. We attended concerts at the Park, which were held in the canteen.

The canteen was just outside the park gates on Wilton Avenue and depending on the shift pattern I either ate there or at my billet. Food and board was paid for by the army so my pay could be used for toiletries, cinema and chocolates depending on what was available in town.

When I was billeted in Loughton with the Foxley family, eating there was far more preferable to eating in the canteen. There were five family members and three of us ATS girls all adding to the rations. The family also had a fruit and vegetable garden so there was plenty of food for us all.

Once, while at Loughton, I remember oversleeping. In my rush to catch the bus to the Park I ran down the stairs without my skirt and had to make a hasty and embarrassed retreat to hide the army issue khaki knickers. Luckily the bus had other village collections to make so once dressed, I walked the fifteen minute journey to the A5 to catch the bus at its next stop.

Once the military camp was built to house the increasing workforce, I moved along with many others to the camp on Shenley Road, situated north of the park. The camp came under the command of Lt. Col Fillingham. It was made up of a series of huts designed to house about eighteen people but ended up with thirty beds to each one. They were built from breeze blocks and bitumen floors. Each hut had two stoves fuelled with wood and coke. They were very difficult to fire and caused an awful lot of smoke, which was almost worse than being cold! The chimneys were unprotected so we had to be very careful not to touch them. Because of these hazards, we often didn't light the stoves – instead we would have a hectic game of table tennis just before bed time and rush under the covers while our circulation was at its best.

We had three square palliasses each. In order to reduce the risk of falling into the gaps onto bare boards as they slithered and slipped during the night, we sacrificed a blanket in which to 'parcel' the palliasses.

Food was served in the mess, which was mixed so men and women ate together. The separate ablutions block had concrete floors and duck boards to stand on by each wash basin. We were only allowed four inches of water in our baths! The camp had a perimeter fence but in the hot summer we would take our bedding into a nearby field to cool down. Once or twice we even slept there and made a hasty retreat back to our huts in the morning. We never got caught, but then our hut was the last hut nearest the field.

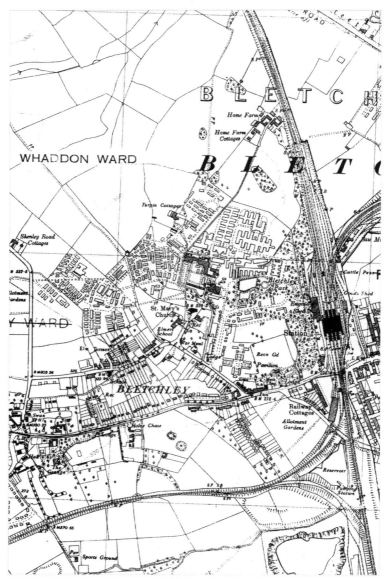

Post war Ordnance Survey Map © Ordnance Survey

Chapter 6

Washington D.C

John Burrows & Charlotte Vine-Stevens, Washington 1945. © Charlotte Webb

It was May 1945, the European war was over but there was still work to be done. The war with Japan was still in progress and our attention was moved towards sending staff to work in Delhi.

Along with twenty others, I reported to Company Office for an interview to assess my suitability for Delhi. I was selected but I somehow knew I would not be going even though my name was on the deployment list. I had a strange premonition, which has not been uncommon in my life, convincing me that Delhi was not to be my next destination.

The next day Don Parkin, Head of the Japanese Section, told me I would be going to Washington. In fact, I would be working in the newly constructed Pentagon building. I felt both honoured and excited especially as I was the only member of the ATS to be posted there – a humble staff sergeant!

After a short embarkation leave I travelled to Euston Station and took the bus to the War Office Holding Unit, ATS, 12 Radnor Place, London located near Hyde Park. The unit was effectively a holding camp for army staff waiting for deployment outside the country. Notably, Winston Churchill's youngest daughter, Mary Spencer-Churchill, was stationed at the unit towards the end of the European war as an ATS Junior Commander.

It was Whitsun 1945 and the first holiday since the outbreak of war that people were able to visit London without the fear of bombings. This visit was no holiday for me: the officer responsible for my movement order was on weekend leave and the relevant envelope lay unopened on her desk. I had no option but to wait at the holding centre, sleeping in basic accommodation while I waited for further instructions.

Following a telephone call to Don Parkin to explain why I was still in London, he quickly arranged for me to be seen by another department in the War Office. The problem was soon resolved and I was sent on a train to Poole to catch a Sunderland flying boat to Baltimore.

Getting onto the flying boat meant a very choppy ride in a small boat from the harbour and then unceremoniously clambering onto the Sunderland's wings to get on board.

This was my first flight and I was extremely scared of taking to the skies in such uncertain times. Who knew what would be waiting for us up beyond the clouds? I was also unnerved by the anonymity of the civilian clothes worn by my fellow passengers. I was in uniform, but the other passengers (all male) were wearing civilian clothes, which made me more nervous because I feared they might ask me what I was doing and where I was going. Fortunately, none of them spoke to me. I must have been a most unattractive travelling companion as I was quite unable to stop my sickness, even though the pilot kindly gave me some pills: they didn't help!

The first stop was somewhere in Ireland to refuel and eat. It was dark and I felt too ill to eat or enquire where we were. We climbed back aboard the Sunderland to find the seating had been rearranged so that we could lie down and sleep. We soon took off again and continued to fly due east for what seemed to be an endless sleepless night. Finally, we came down through a beautiful morning mist to land at Botwood, on the Canadian island of Newfoundland.

We looked out over a vast expanse of fir trees as we ate breakfast at the airport. I was amazed to see bacon and eggs on the menu and found it ignited my appetite. I happily ate the bacon and eggs as well as trying Grape-Nuts, which is a breakfast cereal that neither contains grapes nor nuts but is actually made from wheat and barley. The breakfast worked wonders at easing my travel sickness and finally I was able to enjoy our flight south west over the United States of America to Baltimore.

Feeling weak and tired I was relieved to get out of the Sunderland at last. Captain John Burrows from my section, at Bletchley Park who had selected me to go out to Washington, met me at the airport and escorted me on the final leg of my journey to Washington. Years later I asked John why he had chosen me for Washington. He simply answered *"because I thought it was a good idea"*.

I was relieved when he took me straight to my billet at the Cairo Hotel on 16th and Q in Washington to finally get some sleep before starting work the next day. I quickly found my room, which I was to share with Pip Wallace, another ATS girl who came from Hull. I didn't know it then on that first night, or was too tired to care, but the hotel was very uncomfortable and did not have air-conditioning. The oppressive 100 degree heat, high humidity and constant battle with the thriving cockroaches in my room were the only drawbacks of my five month stay in the capital city. Pip turned out to be a very good cockroach catcher, which was a good thing since every night we had to kill as many as possible before we could go to bed wrapped in bath towels to combat the sticky heat.

The next morning I dressed in my uniform, quickly realising that I would be perspiring from the moment I did up the last button of the woven jacket designed for British weather. Before long I was issued with a light Canadian summer uniform which included nylons that felt so light compared to those issued at home, but on that first day, I had to endure my own heavy kit.

I left the hotel and caught the designated bus travelling to my new place of work, the Pentagon. Travelling for the first time like a wide eyed sightseer, I gazed out of the window marvelling at the city as we took the thirty minute journey over the Arlington Bridge and Potomac River into the state of Virginia, where the Pentagon is sited. Although technically it is in Arlington, Virginia, the Pentagon is addressed as

Washington DC (District of Colombia). It was on these bus journeys that I experienced segregation for the first time - the African American travellers were confined to the back of the bus.

The enormity of the Pentagon building is hard to describe. Compared with today there was lots of open space around it so it stood proudly out of the landscape. Situated over five floors, the offices started on the first floor above the ground level car park. The bus drove straight into the car park where I was met by John Burrows who escorted me to a meeting with the Section Head.

The Pentagon is enormous – a far bigger operation than I had experienced at Bletchley Park. The Pentagon was built quickly to cope with the growing demands of the growing government War Department. On 15 January 1943 the vast site spanning over 34 acres was complete.

From the car park escalators took the thirty two thousand workers, who passed through the building over a twenty four hour period into a vast busy concourse. The concourse had shops, a bank, medical centre and church. Security was tight and access to the concourse was only granted upon the presentation of your pass to the US Army personnel stationed at each access point. The same procedure was then followed outside each office and it was checked every day without fail. I remember I was friendly with one of the American girls who checked the passes and one day I asked in frustration if she really needed to check my details. She still checked my details and did so every day that I worked in the building.

Colonel O'Connor was the American Section Head whose staff included John Burrows, James Pope-Hennessey (later, Queen Mary's biographer), me and others from other US and UK services. I seem to recall that the majority of general staff were women and we worked in a large open plan office accessed via a ramp from the main concourse.

I had a desk and typewriter where I was tasked with paraphrasing intelligence reports derived from the intercepted Japanese communications from Burma. Although the four year Burma campaign was effectively at an end by the time I arrived in Washington, the Japanese forces did not surrender until the end of August 1945. The process of paraphrasing was identical to my duties at Bletchley and although I don't remember exactly the contents, I do recall there was a constant flow of signals passing between Japanese forces which kept me busy between my work hours of 9am to 5pm.

There were many British personnel on duty in Washington and we were well integrated with our American allies. We were required to visit the British Embassy and sign the visitor's book. By way of acknowledgment we all received visiting cards from HM Ambassador and the Countess of Halifax. I still have mine.

Sometimes my duties involved being a Special Courier of secret papers from one department to another within Washington. To me, that was scary. I remember clutching the precious documents to my person and was greatly relieved having delivered them without incident.

At work I often took lunch with my American colleagues and we had the choice of where to eat as food was served in canteens as well as outside in the five acre open air area in the courtyard at the building's centre. This was the area where General Dwight Eisenhower drove round in a tank when he returned from Europe after the end of hostilities. Despite its size, the temperature of the central area took your breath away in contrast to the cool air-conditioned building so I preferred to eat my lunch inside.

Lunch time in the central courtyard of the Pentagon. ©Department of Defence

Of all the food I ate, I mostly remember the salads which included watermelon. Although common place today they were a complete luxury to me after all those years of rationing. Rationing was minor in comparison to the level I experienced at home. However, there was some rationing of meat, which was exchanged for small tokens.

There were no catering facilities at The Cairo Hotel so all my meals were taken in cafes or restaurants. I paid forty four dollars a month for my room and I was paid an extra five dollars a day for food which was ample for covering my eating expenses. Food was not scarce; as soon as you sat down in the booth at a restaurant a waitress would bring out a jug of water and large lettuce leaf piled with cottage cheese to eat while you waited for the main course. I remember that you could deposit a nickel in a slot and select a record to be played within the booth.

Off duty I mostly mixed with British friends, either to eat out, go to cocktail parties at the flats of those fortunate to have them, concerts or the occasional visit to the ballet. Even in those days we were advised not to go about un-escorted in the evenings. Our chaps were very helpful in this and always made sure we were seen back to our billets. I wore civilian clothes when off duty, which were cheap to buy but did not seem to be made of the same quality as those I had at home. Not that I minded, as again it was a pleasure to explore the department stores and have choices that were not available in the time of frugal rationing at home.

I got on well with my roommate Pip: we had formed a strong bond over our cockroach annihilations. Pip had short dark hair and a pretty, friendly face and had a fun personality. We only met up in the evenings back at the hotel as she did not work in the Pentagon. I know she was a Private in the ATS but I did not know what she did in Washington.

In the autumn I did manage to get away from the city for a weekend with my American friend (who checked my pass each morning at the office door). We travelled by train to her family home near Providence in Rhode Island. Again the contrast with the train journeys I had taken in England was remarkable – there were no blackouts, no crowding or sleeping on the floor. We did have an uncomfortable situation with a drunken GI pestering us, but the train guard soon moved him so we were able to enjoy our journey in peace. I remember how beautiful the countryside looked in the rich autumn colours and the fields of ripening corn. We spent a fabulous weekend roasting marshmallows on the barbeque and taking a tour by car to explore a landscape untouched by war.

At the end of the war with Japan, I was working in a British Joint Services Mission office and there met Commander Denniston's daughter, Margaret, known as 'Y'. We became friends and the last time we met was in 2005 just before she died. I do miss her.

On the morning of 6 August 1945 the atomic bomb was dropped on Hiroshima. The authorities intercepted a message indicating that Japan would never surrender and the decision was made to take the action that would finally turn the tide of war. On the 9 August 1945 a second bomb was dropped on Nagasaki. I will never forget hearing the news. Everyone in Washington (and no doubt the rest of the USA) 'went crazy' – continuous blare of car horns and tearing around the city, shouting and waving. I joined a crowd who thronged around the White House calling 'We want Harry' (Harry Truman who was President of the USA at the time). I didn't truly understand the impact the bomb would have on Japan nor the lasting effects of radiation on future generations. At the end of a long war, it meant we were winning and on 14 August 1945 Japan finally surrendered.

Up to that point food had been rationed in the States, although not as rigidly as it was in UK. Steaks were difficult to come by, BUT on the day the bombs were dropped, steaks appeared in the restaurants as if by magic! The celebrations went on all night; such excitement and the noise from hundreds of car horns drowning everything else.

Chapter 7

Back to Bletchley

The war with Japan was finally at an end and the world was once again returning to a peace. It was October 1945 and time for the British Forces in Washington to return home. While waiting for my movement order I moved to a building near the White House to help out with general tidy up duties. Security was still tight and if I went shopping at lunchtime I had to show the guards everything I had bought, which could be embarrassing if it involved personal items. It was also time to hand back the light Canadian uniform and return to my official ATS uniform in preparation of the return to England. I managed to hang onto the light stockings, which caused much envy when I finally returned home.

Those last days held opportunities to do some shopping to buy lots of clothes and gifts for my parents. I filled my two issue kit backs and ended up obtaining a further two kit bags, which seemed a good idea until I had to carry a bag under each arm and one in each hand upon arrival in New York.

It was 5 October 1945 and I was to be in charge of a few other ATS girls for the duration of the journey to England. We travelled on an English cruise ship, Aquitania, which had been requisitioned as a troop ship. It was in a rough, battered state and even though the travelling conditions were little more than basic, it was hard to dampen my excitement at going home.

On arrival in New York we were told the Stevedores (porters) were on strike, meaning we were stuck in New York.

However, it gave us the opportunity to see something of New York, including a production of 'The Importance of Being Earnest' by some local nuns who sounded more English than we did – it was hilarious. I also went to the ballet, "Ballet Russe Highlights", choreographed by Leonide Massine. It was a collection of short ballet highlights, including a memorable one titled "The Dentist". The furious rain prevented me from really taking in the sights but the unexpected stay in New York was very enjoyable and was made possible by the additional pay allowance of seven dollars per day (we received five dollars in Washington).

Eventually, we were on board, but having to carry our own luggage. I spent most of the first two days sitting on deck enjoying the glorious weather. Despite the greater feelings of relaxation, it was impossible not to have thoughts of unexploded sea mines. The Atlantic turned nasty and for the remaining three days to Southampton I was very sick and stayed below in rather basic conditions. It was a great relief to disembark! The MPs at Southampton kindly took me and the other ATS girls through a side door avoiding Customs and put us on a train for London where I felt relieved to finally arrive at the holding unit at Radnor Place. In my excitement to be back I thought of calling on my friend Angela Lenton, so rushed into her office, only to find myself face to face with Mary Spencer-Churchill, the Prime Minister's daughter, a Junior Commander in the ATS. She smiled sweetly as I backed out in embarrassment saying 'Very sorry Ma'am'.

From Radnor Place I was sent back to Bletchley, where I arrived as they were shredding paper and dismantling machinery. I have no memory of how long I was there waiting for a new posting, I just remember the atmosphere one gets after everyone has gone home from a party or a feeling of emptiness after packing a house up before a move.

My stay must have been only for one or two nights at the Shenley Road Camp, where I remember eating a meal. I was not required to help the few people left to pack up the site so I felt a little lost and, it is sad to say, it was almost an anticlimax in comparison to the bustle and focus which had filled the place during the war years.

For me, the war was over. I had one last night at Bletchley before I was posted to East Grinstead to wait for discharge from the Army (demob). My demob group to come up in February 1946 and finally I could go home and spend time with my family.

Chapter 8

Post War Years

Armed with a 'nest egg' of £52 and clothing coupons, I went back to the family smallholding, Ryecroft, to help out. The war years must have been a great strain on my parents, as it was for thousands of others of that age group. There was a collective air of sadness for the loss of loved ones, loneliness and uncertainty. Not to mention the daily struggle caused by food and fuel shortages.

My war years were relatively comfortable and interesting. Bletchley Park was for me the next best thing to a University – exploring a new found independence and living amongst a cross-section of interesting people. In my view, it was a unique establishment and a unique experience. I am sure such a gathering could never be repeated!

Life moved on and so did I. The government paid for my six months secretarial course in London from late 1946 to Easter 1947. A dreadful winter – everywhere was frozen up, and the food and fuel shortage had not eased. Some of my fellow students fainted from the cold. I had dared to attend in a pair of Army issue trousers (dyed plum) and was sent for by the head. I was given a strict telling-off for appearing in such garb, which she described as *'quite unsuitable for young gentlewomen'*. I pleaded with her, reminding her that travelling on an unheated train to and from Croydon each day warranted some protection. I got away with it on the understanding that the minute the weather improved, a skirt would be worn!

We were well taught in shorthand, typing, a language of our choice (I took Spanish), how to write business letters and all the etiquette rules in connection with invitations and replies. We also received some guidance in stock market dealings (way over my head!) and I came away with my only qualification - a RSA first class in Typing.

Cousin Rosemary Harris was on the same course and sailed through everything with top marks as she always did, and with her degree (BA) in, I think, Latin and Greek, she soon had a job as Personal Assistant to the Head man at the NIRD (National Institute of Research Dairies) at Reading University where she remained for forty seven years and was awarded an MBE for her work there.

Adjusting to the post-war years was difficult. Many had had their education/training interrupted. Food shortages and rationing was with us until 1953. For me, those initial post war years held another obstacle. Due to my obligations under the Official Secrets Act, I was not allowed to tell any prospective employer what I had been doing for the previous four or five years. Luckily, the then Head of Ludlow Grammar School had been at Bletchley himself so I had no difficulty in getting in there on the office staff. It was definitely a case of 'who you know' as distinct from 'what you know'.

Then by chance, because of my continued friendship with John and Margaret Borthwick which had begun in 1946 when I lived with Margaret's Aunt and Uncle Hancock whilst attending the secretarial course, I stumbled on a job with Messrs Williams & Williams, Metal Window manufacturers in Chester where John Borthwick was Managing Director. I was employed by Mr Tom Sarl-Williams as part of a team of five secretaries and dealt, mainly, with Staff Pensions.

There, I met another employee June Solloway, who had also been at Bletchley and we became good friends (and are to this day) and through her husband, who was a member of the 4th Battalion, the Cheshire Regiment – TA, I became an Officer of 321 (Cheshire Battalion) WRAC (TA). Mr Sarl-Williams was in favour of the TA and readily gave me time off to attend the annual TA camps (with pay). We shared the Drill Hall in Volunteer St Chester with the Cheshire Regiment and were even welcome in their Officer's Mess. It was jolly crowd of men – mostly local Solicitors, Land agents, etc. So the social life was good – lots of cocktail parties, dances, etc. and the great occasion when Her Majesty the Queen presented new Colours to the 4th and 7th Battalions on the Chester racecourse in 1957 followed by a splendid Ball which went on till 4am.

In Autumn 1959 I was invited to take the position of PSO (Permanent Staff Officer) to 321 (Ches) Bn. WRAC.TA, with the rank of Captain, Adjutant to the Commanding Officer Major Margaret Southern, which I did and stayed there until the re-organisation of the T.A. in 1961 when 319, 320 & 321 Battalions were amalgamated and the HQ set up in Southport. It was all very sad and I hated Southport.

Mummy visited me here: she was very ill and died a few weeks later in Hereford General Hospital. I was in Scotland at Camp near Gleneagles, but managed to get to the hospital in time to be with her before she died. However, I doubt if she knew I was there with Daddy and Margaret.

We were all shattered and saddened by Mummy's death – I had no idea how to come to terms with life without her and was not helped by my Commanding Officer's hard response to my tears: she said '*I didn't cry when my mother died*'. Dad's distraught state convinced me to ask for a posting to Bristol which made it easier to get to Monkerton House, near Leominster, where Dad lived, if I was needed.

Charlotte Vine-Stevens in Territorial Army uniform,
mid 1950s © Charlotte Webb

So eventually I moved to Bristol and was able to go by train to Leominster and give Dad a little moral support more easily. He was totally 'lost' without Mummy but insisted I should carry on with my life in the Army. Life does have to go on, we have no choice.

My years as a full-time TA Officer brought me into contact with people from all walks of life from the very humblest to the very highest in Society. I was apprehensive when faced with meeting the Duke and Duchess of Beaufort in the sixties. They were both very active in the Bristol area and the Duchess became our Honorary Colonel (71 Bristol Coy WRAC (TA)) and as such she visited our premises and the Mess and hosted the company at Badminton House for a training weekend. I slept in the Duke's old bedroom in a brass bedstead with a red silk bedspread. The walls were adorned with photos of his Eton days.

I need not have been afraid – the Duke and Duchess were very kind to us and easy to talk to. I will never forget the Duchess reminding me of the collective name for goldfinches and when she joined us at TA camp in Folkestone I asked her if she would like breakfast in bed – *'Oh no, Betty, thank you, I hate crumbs in bed!'* was her reply.

It was the Duchess who presented all our officers with a shield when the company was disbanded in 1966. Mine is proudly displayed in my hall above my 'Bletchley – Freedom of the Park' parchment.

At the other end of the scale were those I enlisted into the Regular WRAC and QARANC whilst working as a Recruiting Officer for the West Midlands from 1966-1969. I interviewed the applicants in Birmingham, Stoke-on-Trent (Hanley), Shrewsbury, Worcester, Hereford, Wolverhampton and Coventry – a very mixed bag of accents and attitudes, rich and poor, educated and not so. My time at Bletchley, Washington and the Army had given me the skills to communicate and engage with people from all backgrounds with respect and compassion. It is all those experiences that made me good at my job and I never forgot the value of discretion.

During that time I drove or was driven to the above towns from Birmingham on a weekly basis. So I have grown up with some of our major road developments, particularly the ring roads in Birmingham, the M5, 6 and 42. Driving was more of a pleasure then. Now it is so very hazardous; the volume of traffic and drivers' lack of consideration and sense of danger. My driving experience dates back to the late 1940s and includes some appalling weather conditions during the winters of 1963/4 and others.

I left the Army in September 1969 for a post as Area Secretary to the YWCA, which I had expected to ensure me a pension (The Army had not, because my commission was as a Territorial as distinct from a Regular Officer). The move turned out to be a disaster – I did not understand it and was most unhappy. However, Alfred and I had met in 1968 and Daddy was having trouble with his eyesight – two good reasons to leave the YWCA for happier times.

Alfred Webb and I married on 18 July 1970 in Leominster on a lovely sunny day with a small party of family and friends in the garden of my father's home, Monkerton House, Stoke Prior. After that, Alfred and I, and dog Prince, motored to Yorkshire for a week.

We were destined to have only nine and a half years together; they were good years for me, very different being a wife and housewife after all the varied experiences of my previous life. It was an irony that Alfred had survived the War in the Army (Guards Armoured Division) in Europe without a scratch to be diagnosed with hardening of the arteries in 1976 at the age of fifty seven.

The medics at the Queen Elizabeth Hospital did all they could to keep him alive but it was not to be and with hindsight, I think Alfred would have hated life as an amputee. I was shattered, of course, and it took me a long time to come to terms with life without him. Colin, Alfred's son from a previous marriage, and his family lived nearby and were a great comfort as were his other sons Ian, Pete and their families. I am very lucky to have shared happier times with my extended family.

Fortunately, my job at Birmingham Law Society was kept open for me and I returned to a job where I was happily employed for sixteen years as Administrative Secretary with a staff of twelve and being responsible to the Council. I also found new hobbies, including weekly Norwegian lessons given by Mrs Veslemoy Lunt, (whose husband Canon Ronald Lunt was head of King Edward's School, Birmingham).

The Norwegian lessons introduced me into another interesting mix of people – some with direct Norwegian connections, others, like me, just learning Norwegian and Norwegian culture, simply because we were interested. I learnt that Canon and Mrs Lunt met in Norway in the early days of the War when he was parachuted in with our Forces. I also met ex-Bletchley WREN, Joan Martin. Her son is married to a Norwegian and as the local choir master in Straume, near Bergen, brought the choir to Birmingham. We entertained them and made more friends. One of the families entertained me in Norway in 1992 and I still write to them at Christmas time.

Norway is beautiful and I'm glad I was able to speak a little Norwegian, as I felt those we came in contact with were pleased to hear some of the English making an effort! In my view, to say English is spoken everywhere you go is neither true nor the right attitude. We are lazy about learning other languages. It is a pity because this attitude means we miss out on so much. When people ask me *'Why Norwegian?'* my reply is *'why not?'* I find it fascinating although it's sometimes similarity to German gets me into trouble with Norwegians, who understandably prefer not to be associated with their one time invaders.

All through my working life since joining the ATS in August 1941, I have wondered how I would be 'rated' by others for not having had conventional schooling. 'PNEU Homeschool' doesn't always mean anything unless fully explained. However, I believe there are a small minority of people who were educated thus and like me, have managed to cope. Despite my worries and something of an inferiority complex, I succeeded in staying with various employments and generally 'holding my own' socially. To this day my heart always sinks when someone says *'Do you remember how it was at school?'* but now I have plucked up courage to say *'No, I do not, because......'.*

I gained enormous confidence during 2005-2006, being thrown in at the deep end as Consort to my friend Jill Dyer, who was Chairman of our District Council and as such accompanied her to a great variety of Civil, Social and Business functions – about one hundred and fifty in all. A most interesting and rewarding experience AND a great privilege and honour. The highlight of the year was attending a garden party at Buckingham Palace on 19 July 2005. We were chauffeur-driven to London in the very luxurious official car and after a delicious lunch at the Goring Hotel in Beeston Place, we joined the crowd of nine and a half thousand people in the gardens at the rear of the Palace. Entrance is through the Palace, passing through the Ballroom. Everyone was obliged to verify their identity to the Palace guards by showing their passports, driving licences and a recent bill with full name and address. Afternoon tea consisted of beautifully presented sandwiches, cakes, ice-cream and iced coffee or other non-alcoholic beverages served by faultless young men and women in immaculate dress.

The guests were also very formally dressed – the ladies in fabulous colours and of course, hats, the men in either military uniforms or morning dress, Chains of Office where appropriate. All added to the spectacle. Her Majesty the Queen, Prince Philip, the Duke of Kent, Prince Charles and the Duchess of Cornwall and the Duke of York mingled with the guests. Sadly, because of the numbers, we did not see Her Majesty at close quarters.

In recent years I have served on Wythall Parish Council as a Parish Councillor. I have been surprised and delighted that so many local groups, of one sort and another, invite me to speak to them about Bletchley Park, the National Codes Centre, my time there and its war time function. Giving these talks is most enjoyable for me and I am impressed by the amount of genuine interest in the subject.

It has not always been easy to talk about Bletchley, even after the veil of secrecy was lifted in July 1975. It took until about 1994 for me to open up about my experiences, when a friend suggested I give talks. My first talk was to his Probus Club and the talk was a hit. Since then I have talked to groups of about thirty to forty people but sometimes to in excess of a hundred people at a time. From retired people to a group of school children it seems that Bletchley Park has captured the imagination of the nation. I not only talk about Bletchley's past but its evolving future as a museum that is open to the public. New information regularly comes to light from veterans and documents released into the National Archives, further enriching Bletchley's story.

Below is my father's report on the abandoned British Legion Police Force mission to Czechoslovakia (see Chapter 3).

BRITISH LEGION AGM
LUDLOW
21 October 1938

As a very ordinary member of the British Legion, it is a great honour to have to give an account of the all too brief life of the Volunteer Police Force, which was created almost at a moment's notice for service in Czechoslovakia. It may be called an offspring of the Legion and though it died so young, it was indeed a very sturdy child – as the events from October 5th to 15th go to prove.

To go back a few weeks to about the middle of September – the F.O. asked our National Chairman if he could raise a force of 10, 000 legionnaires should they be required.

You have no doubt about his reply.

Later, political circumstances changed the whole situation and Sir Francis Fetherston-Godley was asked again by the F.O. if he could create a body of 1200 Volunteer Police from the Legion for service at once in the Plebiscite area.

On Wednesday Oct 5th all branches received memos calling for volunteers. As time was pressing, the onus was put on the County Secretaries, who were to have the application forms before 6 o/c that evening.

The result was that in two days, 17, 000 applications had been received and the Force of 1200 complete and equipped was ready to sail on Friday night. Three days after the memos were sent out from H.Q.

On arrival at Olympia, each man received his identity card and then filed into his contingency site, one of the two galleries round the

Empire Hall. After being well satisfied by Messrs J. Lyons & Co, each man filled a canvas Palliasse and pillow with straw and drew 2 blankets (or more). After which it was not long before every man had received his blue suit and badge, belt, stick, gloves and Legion tie, haversack, water bottle, 2 shirts, 2 towels and cleaning materials. Metropolitan police great coats and caps, the next morning, completed the issue.

The Force had its own fleet of Bedford Motor Vans and motorcycles for despatch riders and a St Johns Ambulance unit.

On the Saturday morning, the whole Force marched out with the Band of the Welsh Guards. The Legion standard bearer alongside the Guards Colours made a fine show. The O.C. addressed the Force in Empire Hall after the parade and expressed his appreciation of the performance. Twenty years after demobilization (from the First World War 1918) and every man marching with a swing. He added the main point of the march was to see if the boots pinched!

Sir Philip Morris also gave the Force a cheery address and told how he had flown over to see Herr Hitler who cordially welcomed the scheme and said when the BLVPF was used in the Plebiscite areas, German troops would <u>not</u> be employed. On this occasion too, General Sir Ian Hamilton mounted a trestle table and gave his welcome and was greeted with the most tremendous cheers.

Lady Spencer Churchill, who had taken charge of the comforts of the men, had a great reception when she announced that she had rung up Imperial Tobacco Co and asked for 60, 000 cigarettes "on tick". The reply was "<u>no</u> tick, you can have them".

Epilogue

A Great Honour

On 9 October 2009, a little over fifty nine years since my October return to England from Washington, I was honoured to attend Bletchley Park as one of the thirty five veterans invited to attend the ceremony to celebrate the new Commemorative Badge awarded to all the surviving Bletchley Park veterans. Presented by the then Foreign Secretary, The Right Honourable David Milliband, it was truly a day to remember and it filled me with pride to know that I had served my country in a way that is honoured and remembered today and will continue to inspire future generations.

Charlotte Webb's receiving the Commemorative Badge at Bletchley Park 2009
Crown Copyright – used with the permission of the Director, GCHQ

GLOSSARY

ATS	Auxilary Territoral Service – the women's Army.
Block F	One of largest blocks, which was first occupied in November 1943.
FO	Foreign Office
GC&CS	Government Code and Cypher School
Hut 4	Codebreaking hut built in 1939 to house the Naval Section until it moved to Block A in 1942. The Military Section took over the hut but not the name.
NAAFI	Navy, Army, Airforce Institutes providing catering facilities such as canteens, shops etc
NIRD	National Institute of Research Diaries
PNEU	Parents National Educational Union
PSO	Permanent Staff Officer
QARANC	Queen Alexandra's Royal Army Nursing Corps
RAF	Royal Air Force
RCAF	Royal Canadian Air Force
TA	Territorial Army
WAAF	Women's Auxiliary Air Force
WRAC	Women's Royal Army Corps (replaced the ATS on 1 February 1949)
WRNS	Women's Royal Naval Service, often referred to as WRENS
YWCA	Young Women's Christian Association

INDEX